# TO FLY ONCE MORE

Alice Gorton Hart

Logan, Utah
1988

**Library of Congress Cataloging-in-Publication Data**

Hart, Alice Gorton, 1932-1987.
    To fly once more / Alice Gorton Hart.
    128 p., 16 × 23.5 cm.
    ISBN 0-87421-136-0 : $15.00
    I. Title.
PS3558.A6756T6   1988               88-16337
811'.54—dc 19                       CIP

Book Design: R. P. Bissland
Etchings: Adrian Van Suchtelen

Copyright © 1988
George E. Hart and sons

Distribution and Sales by
Utah State University Press
Logan, Utah 84322-9515

These poems of Alice Gorton Hart (1932-1987) are dedicated by her husband and sons to her many friends who helped develop and sustain her love of poetry, art, and life.

# CONTENTS

## HANDS ACROSS THE VALLEY

## SACRED SPACE

# ACKNOWLEDGEMENTS

Many people have been touched by Alice's poetry and many people helped (both directly and indirectly) in bringing this book to fruition.

Her parents, Douglas and Gee Gorton, are foremost. They gave her the ideal of a quality life, balancing creativity with friendship. A gift from Gee made the publication of this volume possible. Veneta Nielsen, John Patrick, and Richard Schuster taught her love of literature. Two correspondence groups—the Prisms Circle and the Circle of Exchange—sustained this love. Adrian Van Suchtelen guided her artistic efforts, while Lynne Goodhart, Alice Perkins, and Alexa West gave meaning to Alice's strong interpersonal feelings that permeate her poems. Kit Flannery and Ev Kramer added zest to her love of life and to her tennis game. The Journal Group shared her love of journals and added a rich dimension to Alice's personal writing.

In the actual making of this book, the following people were invaluable: R. P. Bissland (design), Gwen Haws (typing and editing), Veneta Nielsen (poetry selection and foreword), Adrian Van Suchtelen (etchings), and Alexa West (editing and spark plug).

Tennis friends, B.C. friends, art friends, poetry friends, journal friends, philosophical friends: Alice's friends were as varied as her poems and many of the following poems acknowledge and celebrate the sacred and secular ties of friendship and life.

# FOREWORD

Selection of poems for *To Fly Once More* has been a process of recomposing her own self-portrait from the many poems of Alice Gorton Hart. Perhaps each poet, like W. B. Yeats who wrote in his *Dialogue of Self and Soul* "...because I seek an image, not a book" seeks to create by many images of his experience one image of his own meaning, his own truth. As perceptions describe the five senses, and reflections describe and interpret the reaches of individual mind and spirit, the shaping of verbal forms articulates and defines a poet's conscious, or unconscious, search for a self-knowledge to put the mind at peace, and to magnify it, and grasps at the ultimate intelligence that pervades all Being, living and other human things as well as vegetable and stone.

The poems are grouped here into three aspects of her search. The first section, Where Vision Lives, includes poems of self-examination, self-understanding sometimes generous, always honest, sometimes severe, demanding herself to "write true words," demanding that she create a self that is growing, colored green for, as she declares, "green is never finished," and urging herself to create a verifiable discipline of mind and soul.

The second section, Hands Across the Valley, depicts others as she tried to know and understand them, with compassion, charity, and love. She was aware that critique of the human environment one enjoys or suffers can be as assuring or as devastating as one's own character allows. This author loved or pitied, but rarely in her poems found an unextenuated fault in those she drew.

xii

Section three, Sacred Space, containing her more complex and philosophical poems, speaks a special reach of identification with nature's life-forms not human, and points at her conviction of the unity of all being. Hers was a truly religious awe and admiration for life, here on an ever changing earth, with others and with self. Great poets have patterned this awe and wonder, thought and feeling, in traditional forms to last memorably for centuries. Alice's patterns are generated by their ideas, and create an intense, introspective figure of her quest, lighted by her joy in languages of poetry and other arts.

*Veneta L. Nielsen*

"ODE TO ALICE"  A/P

A Van Suchtelen

# WHERE VISION LIVES

# INVOCATION

Attend
attend to the owl
He moves through new trees
at midnight

His word:

Who
is the Other who moves closer
further away

Who
is the One
within
without
who inhabits the black?

Attend
attend to the owl
at midnight

# DREAM HOUSE

Front door swings open.
We walk in, light welcomes,
streams through huge windows.
Woodsmoke lingers on hearthstones.
A room for music, friends.

Beckoning door opens on north light.
Bookshelves line this room,
a private space to paint, read, write, meditate.

Further door reveals
cool blue walls, a view of river trees,
spread of quilts and pillows,
place for renewal, sleep.

Kitchen glows in southern light.
Herbs bloom on windowsill,
table laid for ceremonial meal,
smells of garlic and fresh bread.

Here is our center, enclosed in safe walls.
Water runs clear, clock ticks earth time
as life settles in eternal now.
We have come home to mind's dream.

# MY OWN ROOM

Prism swept my room with spectrum
clean of guilt. Through pure refracted
sun the day is cleared of pain.

Water-scented wind brushed dust away
from ancient mirrors darkened
by the years of fear.

I stand in the doorway.
"This room is my own," the light
shining, diamond-cut and free.

No more shadowed shapes can bind me,
windows open wide; with new-found
grace, I turn, to many-colored light.

# Deep Journey

Dogs howl, owls screech, crickets cry
at this first birth, death.
Stunned, I wake to empty bed,
dream weight, real cat, heavy beside me.

Curled into half-warm pillows,
I relive dream journey,
the red of it all, birth time.
Rooster crows, cat stirs.

Journey begins in mud.
Acid green, umber, ocher stains
red and white, beginning the process
all over again, night after night.

Earth colors paint outward face,
suntan, black shadowed eyes,
henna to cover the ageing gray,
death leached, no silver peace.

Deep journey into the self—
animals cry, scratch, menace,
kaleidoscope of monster shapes,
resolve into white, black.

# LOOKING AT AN OLD PORTRAIT

There I am in black and white, finished product
of parental love, environment and a fine education,
the fairy-tale princess, every girl's dream,
white-gowned for "the greatest day of her life."

She stands tiptoe to the future,
lost to her own life for awhile,
a "vision of loveliness," everyone said,
"What a beautiful bride."

Is she still here, buried under 30 more years
of nurturing, volunteer work and fat?
Wrinkles line my eyes, my knee sickens,
halts here in an alien land.

Is there anything left of her dreams?
Did she learn to think beyond what's offered
in *Women's Home Companion*? Yes.
We did. We dream, work together now.

# SELF-PORTRAIT: COLLAGE

I must finish it today
before tennis, before lunch
before cookie baking
before they all come home
before dinner, before night.

I started with high hopes.
I drew, cut, pasted, shellacked,
sat and stared at it.
I cannot draw yet.
What can I make out of myself?

Tissue paper, tennis racket silhouette
book jackets, a male authority head
from the *Smith Alumnae Journal:*
agonized issues of my life composed
into an harmonious visual whole.

My edges are sloppy; I work at composition,
the logical geometry of an ordered life
where a square balances a triangle,
enhances a circle, then down there
what dark shape to balance which love?

I started from the outside in.
Should I have begun in the middle?
What can I put in the center?
I draw faces which are not me.
The center is not there.

I reach out my hand for something.
I feel green, commitment to one color,
with me outside looking in.
I make me green in the middle.
Green is never finished.

# A Ghost Talking

Attuned to ancient ritual
a Chinese woman
prayed to her Kitchen God
with the lift of her cleaver.
She was answered with skill,
clean cut on red carrot
plump chicken, her life.
No waste, dinner was tasty if meager.

Now I begin with electric.
Whenever I cook it's efficient,
no time wasted in prayer, no
respect for the come-from, the making,
the made. Dinner is ample and balanced.
They gobble it down with scant thanks.
Nothing remains but debris,
scraps on soiled plates, fit only for dogs.

Coyote howls on the fringe of the hill.
Shall I invite him to live by the fence,
feed on scraps, hear my prayer?

# JADE RING

Jade enclave
   world smoothed to a whole
   sea round
   silent green

I've seen
   light reshaped in a diamond
   spit fire
   fragment the shape of life

Within jade
   color deepens
   to a new white
   in a golden bound

Look into the stone
   one flaw
   announces life
   twist to the perfect round

# UNDERPAINTING

*for Joe Mugnaini*

Lightning shapes sky images.
Can words thunder, control
such vast dimensions,
or can paint form all we know?

I am a poet, but I want to paint.
Words seem poor coinage, slippery,
misused. I see new-minted clarity
of color, eloquence of line.

I like to paint: sensuous texture
of brush strokes, turp smell,
eager hands spattered with gesso,
burnt umber under my nose.

Poetry is austere, black and white.
I crave color, curves, line sweeps,
putty knife loaded with primaries.
Magical images emerge from darks, lights.

I must write, draw, paint,
strike depths where vision lives,
pull lines around one truth:
black, white or rainbow.

# In Praise of Gray

There are times when black
lines even ones etched by love
grate on skin so bleak that
scored soul retreats,
inky octopus, to sea depth.

There are times when white
makes so much noise that
ears ice over, close.
Grazed eyes scream against snow
whiteout, no end to it.

There are times when color
is too much to bear. Rainbows
craze eyes watered by tears.
The gold pool at arc's end
is merely dying, death.

There are times when gray
is the right color:
a wedge of clay, solid
something to draw on, mould,
erase with a damp finger, try again.

# BELONGING

Being in the right place
is like fitting a new skin
over raw places
meeting the other half of yourself.

These few square feet of enclosed air
winding around my soul are mine.
My balcony delivers the moon.
The ocean is not far away.

Dry mountains deviled my past.
Sagebrush smell stained arid nights.
The wolf who knew me
howled from the foothills at dawn.

Here a full moon discovers me,
sea gleams bright promise for new day.

# IN THE STUDY

My sanctuary, retreat: one lamp shines
on polished wood, some dust, unanswered letters
tennis trophies, a wall of books.

Painted owls perch on the walls
among friends' pictures.
A miniature palm survives an alien climate.

My cat visits ceremonially, claws clicking
in counterpoint to pen scratches.
He curls into sleep.

I hear his oblivious breath,
sound heartbeats. Smooth surfaces
book jackets, conceal turmoil

of grief. Curtains open onto black.
Across facades of calm
light footfalls stalk the cat.

# DIALOGUE IN DARKNESS

I.

*Look how the mountains seem to thrust*
*forward with the weight of snow.*
*Sometimes I feel they will fall*
*and crush me.*

Come away from the window
in that flimsy thing,
you'll catch your death.
Spring's coming soon.

*Yes, I know, but still,*
*even after all this time,*
*the mountains daunt me so,*
*walling us in like this stuffy room...*

Ah, love, don't worry.
I'll save you in the circle of my arms.
But now it's getting late,
how about fixing a couple of eggs while I shave?

## II.

*Spring opens room to morning sun.*
*Pale plants stir and stretch in the new light.*
*But I, on too familiar rounds,*
*water listlessly their confined roots*
*and feel no lightening.*
*Is he calling from the garden*
*for a drink of water?*

She didn't hear me.
Thirsty for something unknown, I turn
planting nothing in arid ground.
I watch high mountains flower
feeling dryness below.

## III.

*High noon bakes in desert sun.*
*Sprinkler droplets, diamonds in dry air,*
*are not enough to green this barren land.*
*He cannot understand, born here*
*among the heights and sage, how strange*
*an eastern garden is, vulnerable,*
*out of place and frail.*

She frets so at every season.
But how was I to know the distance
and regret, slow ageing without seed,
her rejection of this land?

## IV.

*Autumn evening wind feels chill*
*blowing down the canyon pass*
*from high snows that never melt.*
*The sense of cold is always with me now,*
*as flowers fade, the garden goes to seed,*
*sun's heat recedes and all light fails.*

I cannot find her in the dark.
The chill of her absence stills compassion.
Now is the death time, rattle of dry stalks.
I sit by a dying fire of green logs
while encircled mountains cup the dark.

# CACHE

This woman is hidden in a valley
between two mountains.
To the south there is an icy pass,
to the north, a road full of fog.

This woman feels the stirring of spring
but she is surrounded by gray snow,
black asphalt, bare trees,
square houses with no private spaces.

This woman carries her own mountain within her,
snowcapped and sparse with juniper.
Sagebrush scrambles for a living on lower slopes.
It is an old mountain and very heavy.

This woman sits in front of her mirror,
combs out her long hair, stares into herself,
sees only the mountain behind her,
reflected in bleak eyes, not her own.

# PLANTINGS

Twelve tomato plants, three geraniums
two cats, two kids, one husband
three plum trees, two norway pines
one blue spruce, a cucumber...

Not my soil, dry clay soaks up water,
makes mud. I skid on surface,
encased in rusting steel, ride
on bald tires along routine roads.

I had a map once when I was young,
an owner's manual, direction.
I'd fly to the sky-shore, watch
sea otters play, cheer thunder,

ride wild surf on a leaky raft.
Now rivers are dirty, bare desert roads.
Tree roots snake-coil on trampled shores.
Floating driftwood stares with alligator
eyes.

# PRAYER TO THE TENNIS GODDESS

May the wind soften and a benevolent cloud hide
the sun when I am playing a match.

When I play mixed doubles, may my partner serve like
Boris Becker, play the net like John MacEnroe, have the
patience of Job and the forgiveness of Jesus.

When I play women's doubles, may our opponents be
little old ladies who don't know how to hit spins.

When I play singles, may my feet be light as water
running, my reach as long as the rays of the moon,
my strategy as subtle and effective as Scheherazade's.

May I never double fault, my bra never break,
my overhead never catch in the net.

May I be tournament tough forever.

# ATONEMENT

I feel so unclean—
but the well is dry
in this year of drought.

I look at my soiled body,
my breast shrunken,
my mouth rigid, eyes afraid
to look at my neighbors
all starched and clean.
Nothing shows on the white linen
of their righteous robes.

Where can they find the water to wash in
when the rivers run low,
no clouds gather, no rain falls
on this stark, parched land?
What healing can they find
to poultice their human souls?

Am I the only one who is stained
with guilt, denied forgiveness?
To be free of this—
I have knelt by the dry well
through the black hours when no tears come.
My cracked lips form the ancient prayer
but no mercy appears.

Yet, when the dark hour is here
alone, I can accept my soul
and nourish the gray rose
with a little water.

# SWEETWATER

You are my river
flowing through arid country.

At the touch of your eyes
my landscape turns green,
scrub sagebrush towers into pine
bleak hillsides blossom with grasses
an oasis of trees.

You dominate my horizon like Mount Hood.
The great river runs like love
through dark canyons in my mind.

I carry the thought of you
within me like a secret well
a precious porcelain bowl
of clear water.

# DOUBLE HELIX

This house is inhabited by devils

They creak the woodwork
   interfere with the furnace
   infest my dreams
   invade my mirror
     with wrinkles and flawed eyes

Who built this house
   to guard what dreams
   of multitudes of sheep and wine
   uncounted progeny
     the warp of what I am

I live here now
   staring through windows
   streaked with rain
   pacing furnished rooms
     strangely foreign yet at home

I'd like to clean house
   throw out unwearable shoes
   photographs of strangers
   outgrown books and dreams
     debris of former lives

I can burn it down

I can let the paint peel
   cracked bricks crumble into ruin
   gardens go to weed
   front porch steps rot
     so no one comes to call

I can live here
   patching what I can against decay
   learning to live with devils
   spending inheritance
     guarding some dream

# ANIMUS

*"If a dog runs at you, whistle for him."*
                    –Thoreau

Something's living in my head
that I can't see.
I suspect a stray beast has crept
into my bone cage.

Can I tame him? Make truce
take him to my heart, trust
welcome invasion
contain his intrusion?

Can I resist him, cast him out?
Find strength, light
clear sight for what is real
to depose him?

Wondering, I hear him prowling—
whisper of claws on stone floor
flicker of tail along bars—
taking possession.

I feel the whistle of his breath,
smell carrion teeth,
sense fear in rising hackles,
the sting of his claws.

# TRANSFORMATION

Stay, sun, let diamond sparkle hoarfrost
be more than ephemeral rime, not change, melt
drip drop by drop—mere water—from winter trees.

Keep delicate beauty, tiny spears, shields
miraculous, bound round black branches...
Stop time's spiral dance, hold loveliness here.

Stay again, this wry rime denies what's real:
dark solstice twig magic must fade till green spears
begin bud-shoot from selfsame spring-changed trees.

# LINES TO SHAPE A NOVEMBER NIGHT

Late night silence—
pen makes no sense.
I trace meaningless lines
with cigarette smoke.

Quiet is behind me,
cold creeps up my backbone
hunching my shoulders,
absence, feel of dead air
in the rest of the house.

To play a tape
would hurt the silence.
Scratch of charcoal on paper
is too much noise.

My bracelets rattle.
I still them quickly.
Bookcases lean toward me
their unread rows, threatening,
as those too well-known.
If I understood perspective
what lines I could draw.

I could draw a thin red line across my wrist.
But that's been done.
No originality there.

A good thought for the turn of the year.

# SHADOW DRAWING: BLACK AND WHITE

## I.

Begin with black shape after midnight,
distorted tree stump, street lamp.
Shadows grow longer, colder, invade sanctuary
crawl under covers, take over once-warm room.

Illumination narrows to frightened eye-slits
watching immobile shadows infest the wall.
Back turned to black, hunched, expectant,
terror overtakes, sucks into dark.

Body cools, ache tightens skin.
Black blots out solace of warmth.
Books ink out of sight, mind chills.
Rats creep over all the graves

## II.

Night fades to gray.
Tree stump returns to tree stump.
Street lamp turns yellow, turns off.
Bright sky
echoes mind lightening:
Black defied for one more day.
Rats scamper back to their lairs.

# BRIGHT CAVE

Black cave mind breeds dreams
where no light lives. Dark seeps
between etched beast lines,
flows uncontrolled
between bones spaced in set design.

Lightening. Rainbow ceiling
takes shape under awakening eyes
still blind with black memory,
mind flooded with nightmare
horror creatures, scaled and horned.

Unicorns come alive on cave walls.
Delicate hooves dance to distant music.
Prism spangled, they prance,
bend with scent of lilacs
laugh shadows from bright cave.

# THE AGED

Not to die before their deaths
somewhere between sanity and otherness—
Chinese sages say holiness comes then
as this fossil shell curled
on itself four million years
knows its own soul,
until it is unearthed
with no fragrance, bone dry
dust drowned.
I polish it and listen
to no sound of sea within:
lost resonance whispers its longing.

# REREADING MY JOURNAL

Just before solstice, dark time of year,
turning inward alone on cold night,
I must inspect where I've been, retrace footprints
not pressed on clean snow, but black scratches
on paper now yellowed with age.

Incessant retreat into words;
philosophy, symbolic logic, semantics,
profound novels, popular psychology,
quotes carefully copied from wise books,
compendium of answers for an ordered life.
I was witty, learned, explained the universe
at the drop of a metaphor.
I had the world by the tail and my pen.
Nothing could color, trip, strip me....

Then, with a look and a touch, love
exploded my black and white world of words
into rainbows, arpeggios, rippling wonders
I tried to write down.
New life wouldn't stay on the page.

Memories abide on aging paper.
Closing the old book I listen to silence
where music still echoes.
My pen marks defy season's first snows.
I must write, shape experience to meaning.
Loves rekindle as I write this.
Life does not yellow with age.

# DISCOVERING LANDSCAPE

Once there were walls all around.
I made gates to the ocean,
climbed slippery sand dunes,
found prickly pears, serene pools.
Tide whelmed offshore.

I moved inland, safe valley,
mountain-ringed.
Encountered earthquakes, mudslides,
avalanches, blizzards, floods.

I escaped to the city-scape:
skyscrapers, man-miracles.
Saw straight angles, crooked ways.

Where to live after such journeys?
Neighbor to myself, I'll fence a garden
open to rain, death, and a tomorrow
of wide sky, imaging air.

# WITCH'S SABBATH

Stare into morning mirror;
you, prisoned in skull's cage,
see vein tracery of blood
on eye whites. Teeth feel
not a part of your face:
grimace of dirty fur.

Last night, composed for sleep
you might have escaped, dreamed
sweet victory in the last, lost war
with love and longing. Instead
spiders slid behind closed eyes.
Snakes, dragons writhed within bone bars.

Before bed, you'd said, "I can handle it,"
spreading thick veined hands
pulsed with pent rage.
They turned to claws in front of your face.
You hid them quickly
in nightgown sleeves.

You chose to dive to visionary depths:
Accept fierce companions.

# SKULL POEM

Coconut with teeth, it sits
top of spine, ribs, pelvis
shaped to elevate it.
Legs, feet carry it.
Arms, hands serve it.

What's inside it? I sit,
feel what's going on inside
but can't name it. Greeks,
wise men, tried taming it.
"Know it," they said.

I think I think inside it.
Something goes on, constantly
goes on. I can't stop it.
There are two sides to it,
Research says. Integrate it.

I can feel the outside bones,
hair, lips, skin of it,
put myriad words inside it,
but it still goes on,
no matter what I think about it.

# LIVING WILL

Cloud-domed, done day behind me,
cricked back aslant, elbows prop
cocked head over these pages:
a good idea here, death with dignity.

Even prophets can't want to linger past living.
Curiosity prompts the reach beyond quickly.
But, when, then, who would say "Over."
Yet, still, wait, there's one more special....

I, piece of Peace, sweet life avow:
Earth's hues, light, shapes, warmth,
cat-life, draped on my shoulder, purr.
Whiskers tickle my chin. Let it be slowly.

# WAITING FOR THE BUS

I care for this telephone pole
gray-brown, weathered by sea winds,
"Bus-Stop" nailed to its side.
It serves several purposes as I do.
We have a lot in common.

I talk to it when we are alone.
I lean against it and say
"Hello, friend, another rainy day.
Thanks for your support,
I bet the bus is late....

You are rooted here
through no choice of your own.
How does it feel
to watch the buses come and go
while you must stand your ground?

Uprooted, processed, trucked here,
tamped in concrete,
is there still some tree inside
with balked desire
to root and leaf once more?"

I put my ear against the pitted smoothness
where bark once was, and listen.
I hear only the approaching bus,
grab for my change,
forget to say goodbye.

# THE OLD POET

This hand of mine must write something

Wrist thickened
Fingers stiff
Nails chipped

I can't care for them now

Once with joy
Pen traced paper

Figures danced
Quick as thought

Light as music
Flowing fountains

Black and white
Patterned delight

Now I hear music

I beat time with my old pen
But the dancers are dead

# HOSPITAL

Do old people cry?
Or are they dry
of emotion's red meat?
Are their shells empty
faded by the sun and sea?

Are they invisible
to youth's unsubtle
blindness to the slow
as they speed in colored flash
tunneling past?

I sit here fingering
my dry and fading hair
and feel its dampness
from a tear.

"HANDS ACROSS THE VALLEY"    A/P

A VanSuchtelen

# HANDS ACROSS THE VALLEY

# LAND'S END

Once, remembered child
inside me, my own past, stood
hand-in-hand with present body
at the edge of a precipice.

We peered north toward Mount St. Helens.
Intently, child me
cupped petal hands over eyes
shook her head.
Even her long-sighted eyes
can't see through the haze.

We have come a long way
from the sandy beach
where we grew up.

Mother says: "You're a big girl.
You can go swimming all by yourself.
Run along now. Don't bother me."

Now, we two, stretched on the sand,
uneasy in our ageing body
stranded on the same beach
weak with our mother's dying
confront ourselves:

We three: Mother Daughter Child
stand between a volcano
and the shore's edge.

# THE RIGHT RIVER

Estuary, semi-salt ebb of rich life
keeps change constant
beneath rough docks
where rockfish live.

Further upriver salmon swim
to one particular sandy bed
to be at the right place
at the right time.

Trout too have their rules of life.
They must swim where there are flies
where fashioned lures entice
catch them from known life.

River weather makes laws for fish.
We came when wind was blowing the wrong way
lines entangled in river weeds,
fish slept behind far rocks.

It was the wrong time for fish
but not for us. As salmon discover
their right river, so did we,
caught together with steel, silk hooks.

Confluence. We swim in our river
float with the tidal flow
celebrate richness along the shore
beware of lures, become fish.

# THINGS TO DO OVER AGAIN

Waken on foggy morning
within sound, smell of ocean shore,
love-warmth curled beside shoulder, thigh.

Wait for the bus at twilight,
arms loaded with treasure
after a long, good day with books.

Watch candlelight brighten my mother's face.
She laughs at my son's joke
like a young girl.

Work on a drawing, absorbed,
pencil alive in my hand.
Each line makes a difference.

Write true words
on a winter night.
Snow whispers communion.

# "IT MAKES NO NEVER MIND ANYMORE"

What makes an always mind
dogs me like a wet Labrador
chasing the wrong stick
down a gray beach at ebb tide.

What she meant who spoke it
eludes me even now, years after
her son died, the meant matter
lost in her grieving mind.

Driftwood thrown out to sea
sometimes returns with spring tides.
Did she recognize the piece
that the dog brought back

carved roughly by winter storms,
fine hewn to no pattern or plan?
"It doesn't matter," she said,
"But it makes a different mind."

# X-RATED POEM

X is a cross shape, slashing angles.
I like circles. As a child
I won with circles at tic-tac-toe,
beating the little boy across the street
the only way I could.
He had an electric train. When he lost
at tic-tac-toe, he'd lock his door.
I lost the only train I ever knew.

X marks which spot, where?
Treasure hunters were always boys,
girls X'd from adventurous existence.
Maps of life shunt women on sidetracks,
no main lines, successful stations.
We trained desire on golden circles
in search of treasure beyond our ranges,
seductive voices luring us to love.

# MEDITATION ON THE MARBLE GAME

My son invented it,
drilled holes in a board,
taught me how to play.
I keep getting sent home.
I hate that. I finally won,
raised my fist in Olympic salute.

Now I can retreat with honor to the study
and think about why I hate this game,
while my other sons play it.
I hear their laughter.

A simple game:
get four marbles around a board.
Risk. Jeopardy, that's it.
I want them to be safe.
These marbles, "men," become my sons.
I want them home safe.

Paradox of motherhood:
if they're good, they're gone.
The world's all wrong:
broken marbles, warped boards.

# PARABLE OF DOMINOES

My small child built a tower of dominoes
Frail and shaky, for he's still young.
I helped him with the balancing.
It almost reached the sky before it fell,
But he was wholly satisfied with its reach
And the delight of its falling.

My older child built the Golden Gate Bridge.
I found the string and scotch tape.
We just have double sixes, so it wasn't very big,
But it was a "groovy" bridge.
We blew on it and it stood firm.
Our knees rocking under the table didn't stir it.
He was disappointed
Because he really wanted it to fall
So we could build a better one.

After the children went to bed,
My husband and I played dominoes,
Placing the numbered counters end to end
As the directions directed
And keeping careful score.

## IDEA OF FUR

She has been textured by the city's edges.
Her once glossy fur, rubbed, tattered, manged,
the truth of loneliness etched on her face
by days when the city wrung her dry
and gave no substance back.

Fog cannot blanket, enclose
hide, warm, comfort her.
It puts grayness in her eyes,
around the hard edges of her elbows:
between her teeth, grittiness.

She showers each morning,
swims in the icy bay, vigorous.
But in her eyes, the cold city lives
hard as the iron fence around her house,
unstable as sand.

She has lost her shine,
the oil on her back
that lets grief run off without drowning.
She scutters from one thing to another
on glassy surfaces, afraid of the water.

# FAMILIAR

*for Kit*

Sheltered, framed, cat purrs,
proud, erect in bright light.
She came through dark fog, present.

I would be witch. I need her.
We take to each other, both strays,
share solitude.

She is my alter ego:
green-eyed, swirl-bodied, provocative.
She summons sunrise and silver.

I would see beyond night window,
incant: "Speak, stay with me."
She knows all the answers.

# DESERT LANDSCAPE

*for Dave and Fran*

I started with blue sky
then mountains
with some snow on brown peaks
a little green,
at the bottom.

What you look at becomes you.
There are two cacti
that look like love
two arms raised, green as peace
balanced, a heartbeat.

There is desolation, a brown desert,
rocks, a suggestion of sage,
I have drawn this picture for you.
I added a blue river with waves.
There are no fish in it.
You will have to find your own fish.

There are empty spaces here.
You will fill them as you must.
I look at it as your lives,
magical, apart, your own,
grounded in what is:
plants, rocks, water,
the green living, loving things.

# WEDDING DRESS

She wanted it, this slim woman my son loves.
My mother sent it, satin preserved for thirty years.
Several spots, mysterious look of rusty time...
speckle the train. They will clean.

I've also aged well, steeped in regulated life,
books, wine, friends, music.
No improper passions have whitened my hair,
ravaged my face, sunk my eyes in desperate contours.

The dress fits her well, my soon-to-be-daughter.
We leaf together through wedding portraits,
images of lost friends, parents, unfinished dreams.
She, eager, laced in love, hugs me.

# Two Kites

Flukey wind
floats mine higher

Your eagle wing
won't beat
my blue
broken-backed
still game
high flyer

Gather in string

Keep tandem
free-flying
stretched tight
kites
striving higher

Drift down blue dying wind

Come to entwined hands
wings fluttering
in sunset wind

# A METAPHOR FOR GEORGE

Color's subdued by my indifferent camera
but not your smile. You sit anchored
to earth, sand, enjoying sky.

In steady sea-wind kite sails far
dips, loops, soars almost free.
Line tautens, sags, Oh! down-plunge.

Sand-scraped, collapsed in sad heap,
kite huddles away down the shore.
You run to the rescue, untangle

lines, sort it all out,
test wind with wet thumb,
give me the signal to fly once more.

# Teaching Beads

*for Ginny*

One perfect amber, amethyst, diamond
after another, she strings for family,
friends. Her hands knot us together.

There are times, days, weeks when
stones break, thread kinks,
her tears weaken (she thinks) the chain.

Her gift, what she is,
shapes her circle of days to more than gems:
herself, her love, her rainbow.

# AGINCOURT REVISITED

We happy few, we band of broken
broads, telling each other's beads
of treasure and regret, we few
have briefly known the nunlike
ecstasy of candles lit against the holocaust,
of shouts across the hurricane,
of whispers that caressed the wind.

Lysistrata thought she knew
the answer to a world at war.
It worked for her time, not ours.
The men we know fight love,
fight tenderness, watch
football on television, reject
our entreaties, die of coronaries.

We must live, for our daughters,
our sons and ourselves. We few,
not happy in battle, must fight for
our loves. Our armor, sweet skin,
our lances, true words, our arrows
of Eros, our bows of belonging,
our winnings, not France, but the world.

# TO A FRIEND

Traditional title evoking
Centuries of witty twistings
Entombed in dusty books

You break erudition's cage
With a rose and a poem

Live grace of green
Fresh thrust of thorn
Firm slim stem

We feel together
What redness means
Scent incarnadine
Of many-petalled love

Poems grow magic too
The soft thrust from mind to mind
Growing a rose
In each mind
Mine worn
Weary of words
Springs green from yours

Sensing you behind the words
Ocean-eyed sun-haired
Graceful greenlike driftwood form
Spare pared-down wave-born

Ready as the rose
For full unfolding
Knowing as the poem
The how and why

Waiting only upon when

# GRANDFATHER

Your eyes see far beyond me.
It is a good photograph
propped here on my desk
in a room you've never seen.
You're here with me
in my bones, heart, memory.

Your daughter
graceful gallant flame-haired girl
is old now,
paring her life down,
passing to me what I need
to keep in touch with you
when she goes where you are.

Your eyes are here now.
Alive, you saw me, loved me
showed me grass shapes
wood charms, star rimes,
the rest of age
and bounty to the young—
who I am, from where I came.

You died in dreadful pain
but still in gentleness.

What you see now I cannot know
I can only hope for you, for me,
for the quenching flame that is your daughter
dying into gentleness as you did
who taught her.

# For My Father

In our perfect universe
George Szell, Jack Nicklaus
rule, greenhouses never
succumb to hail, Esprit sails
well to windward, our limericks scan.

The way it ought to be is
the way we see it,
Andrew Wyeth paints it,
Henry Adams writes it,
Hammond Innes' heroes do it.

The way it is, is the way it
is. Snow, cold, and lungs
too small for great heart,
mind, will: Gorton
stubbornness will win through.

Florida flowers in our minds—
ideal delight, sharing sun, sand
love, laughter—that's the way
it is for us, even now, surrounded
by snow, stark hospital white.

# TWO HORSES

Two glass horses in a velvet case
may hate, may love, may
touch horn to wing, may
bow to each other, fly.

My unicorn has lost his horn
is just a horse, no symbol now
of any flight beyond earth's floor,
his magic drained away.

But still he prances lightly on
four feet, his ears still dance
above arched flow of neck
curved tail reflecting joy.

Your Pegasus still winged, paws air
stands proud with forward eyes
and hearing ears, the lift of love
spreading his frail wings wide.

# LIKENESS

I have captured you
on my white paper.
Limned between lines and spaces
is the long-known, loved look of you.

Your image is in thrall.
Your face, skin, muscle, skull
are known shapes:
eyes speak even when lips are still.

Yet, your essence escapes me.
Innumerable neurons make magic,
never captured, ever new;
beneath your skull lives Mind.

# His Mountain

There you sit
smug hump of stupid rock

He loved you

Don't you know he's dead?
If you didn't kill him, what did?

Someone must watch you
for him
   sunset flows upward
      patterns slope and color
         slips from pinnacle
           is lost
              to the gathering dark

There is no word
There is
Mountain

I am a word woman
   must name it
      bring it inside
        to bear in
But I can't
      won't
            climb it
Until I feel clear

# MAY EIGHTEENTH, 1982

*for Harold Nielsen*

No thunder on the left
for gentle him.
No volcano, on whose birth
two years ago
his death day falls.

Sun shone at times today
though it was right to storm.
We who gathered near
to mourn with her
saw shadows cross the window pane.

We shudder at the sudden violence—
death like lightning strike:
the fierce unknown confronted
in a blasted second
leaving only ash behind.

She, one twisted tree alive,
resists the ashen fall:
volcano hidden in her heart
starkness arrested,
frozen motion,
clock stopped,
in quiet earth where trees begin.

# THREE MUSES

They come to me, hover, comfort:
crone, woman, child,
feathers, golden showers twine their hair.

Haunting, weaving their spells,
Danaë, Leda succumb to incubi.
Transformed, man may know woman.

Can man draw, comprehend the crone?
He may know the child, drape her
in rich robes of blue and white,

enfold her in the black of timeless time,
keep her asleep, safe. But the crone,
the everlast of life, dare he know her?

# Ocean Reef

Submerged coral encloses this safe place.
Palm fronds edge sky lit softly
by star, sand glow. Two dolphins sleep
in their home pool.

We lean over a covered bridge,
watch their serene shapes,
listen in the lustrous night
to whispered breath rippling life

above shimmery water. Your hand,
tanned by lazy days, so dark
I can only feel the touch of it,
licks at my breast as light

as the breath of the sleeping dolphins,
as deep as the sea where they rest.

# ALL THE WORLD'S ...

Curtain: stage erupts in noise.
One large dog, jaw poised at bark,
carpets the boards. TV placed
center stage blares monster movie.
Stereo competes with rock.
Cast sprawled in organized confusion
(no apparent direction)
on rangy sofa left of center
overflows on random chairs.
Speech a cacophonous jungle.

Set designer recreates Middle-American
interior clutter of electronics,
mod pots, unpruned plants in macrame.
Costumes worn casual, jeans, wrinkled shirts
in unmatched shades of green and blue.

Doorbell cues my entrance.

Her tiny spontaneous body
freezes in mid-pirouette, child-face
hid in swing of sun-white hair.
Wide luminous eyes uncover, see me
see something light-flare.
She runs, swings on my instinct arms
outreached, carried up to my shoulder,
head pressed in the sweet spot above my breast.

She smells of love and soap.
I forget my lines, stand dumb
hold this light source
(not in my script, but born for some world)
while all sounds cease and the light burns.

# FOR J.E.B.

Evening deepens as my mind expands
in reading poems of breakage and demand.
Secrets, phantoms, nightmare, all recede.
Sonnet form, beyond me, I concede.

So in the future when I start to write
dream poems with dark and danger, most uptight,
I will re-read, admire, your two quatrains
which do not limp, un-scan or sound too tame.

Now in this poem, I must begin to say
what is the core of brightness seen today:
your face, your voice, your smile, your love, your soul
inspire me to go on and cheer your role.

When your dire cast is off and all is well,
my Prince and yours, my friend, will spin their spell.

# WILSON TWO

Would that love were like a tennis ball:
resilient, discrete, held easily, trustworthy
(until dead) clearly marked
so I could know which one is mine
bouncing on the clouded court.

So sharply etched from concentrated play
that round reality obscures unfocused poems—
the rhetoric, the gaucherie of chimes
off-rimes, the constant beat
of language and the lies.

You write me lines of sweet conceit:
"Barefoot in your springy hair
moonbreath whispers scented dreams."

Faugh! I'd rather have a tennis ball.

# Woodcut Madonna

She again swelling with child
carries her firstborn
astride on her shoulder.
Too old for her teat,
he nuzzles her head
curved apart from white birds.

Her hands, crossing her breast,
steady his foot. She looks afar.
Patient, wary eyes in carved face
endure burden of knowledge,
child who will always be here
etching black lines on her mind.

Gravid with alien being,
charged with fervent unknown,
she smiles: "Messiah I must carry,
cherish, protect. New child,
chosen of my heart's mind,
shall quicken as She must."

# Sphinx Madonna

They rest between Its paws,
no tracks on desert sand,
still night brightened by stranger star,
child's light. She leans on Its breast,
serene face: it is accomplished.

Enigmatic face, chiselled by time,
lifts mystery to dark sky,
lips curved by infinite knowing,
foreseeing, before the word,
still point of the turning world.

# SISTER

Quick
Light
Glancing breeze
Drawing spring scent from winter pine

Still
Gentle
A cool stream moving
Softly over summer stones

Sometimes
Touched with sadness
Frost-muted color of autumn leaves

Her eyes are
Pine-edged pools
Of thought

# AFTER THE PARTY

The last guest is gone

I wander airless rooms
   stained glasses
   cracker crumbs
   spilled wine

It was a good party
Must it be performed again?

All nice people
   all all
   nice people
And I
   no different
   foremost among them all
   Hostess Quickly

   asses bray lions roar
   bottoms up drink again
   dance the Tarot dance the Fool
   scry the universe
   I dare you

Pushing hair from aching forehead
I put a record on

# GIFT OF A CRYSTAL CANDLE HOLDER

*for Veneta*

Candle lit in dark time
throws shadows I cannot draw,
pray to, fathom.
Monet believed shadows have color.
He painted light, shimmer on water.

I light a candle.
Redwood fragrance recalls
deep mystic forest,
well of trees,
Druid drawn,
mythic depth of mind
learning to live with shadows.

Quiet, steady flame
crowns crystal base.
Carved facets reflect light,
rainbow, as she who gave it
draws out the best of me,
transcends shadows, sings.

# HANDS ACROSS THE VALLEY

We reached out—we touched.
The wind began to blow,
Ruffled our hair, our skirts.
We feel clean.

Across the valley, our hands touched.
Springtime, life time,
Easter—a new beginning:
We are cleansed of guilt.

A rain of words, seedtime,
Our minds bear fruit,
Blossom in this new time.
We are one with ourselves.

"SACRED SPACE" 1/1          A VanLuchtelen

# SACRED SPACE

# SACRED SPACE

A different mind builds to a new geometry.
Houses rise, earth roots wrap foundations,
sprout grass, gardens, joy.
Neighborhood street lamps flicker
through wind-danced trees.

Here, then is home:
This body, given for a time to touch the world.
This head which hears, sees, talks, tastes, smiles, cries.
This mind which ranges through dreams, stories, music,
libraries, museums, history, delights in friends.
This soul-spirit whose search is life-long.
The com-munity, this planet.
This galaxy circling through mystery.
This universe....
This is all home, all music, Light.

# Animal Drawing

I live with this fossil shell
paperweight, holding down bills
rejection slips, wedding invitations
birth announcements, letters from friends.
They don't blow away.

I've written poems about this shell.
Heavy with four million years
it lies inert, age-glazed, withstanding wind.
Dormancy, illusive in organic shape
once living, never dead, defies words.

One day, eyes blown child-clear,
I draw the shell shape. Under my hand
it becomes fetus, becomes animal with eyes
fur, claws, curled in the grass.
I see him, light shaped by dark.

I draw a tree for him, shelter from the wind.
He needs some grass to eat.
I draw grass. His nose bends to the grass.
He is alive. I have shaped him alive.
I will draw light inside him, as he is.

# Animal Totems

Eagle appears, circles
soars, disappears to blue.
My eyes are stretched, refreshed.

Stuffed solemn brown bear
protects my bed-cave, connects
to child alive within.

Three frogs, wooden, plush, bronze—
why so many frogs? I leap,
dive deep. Water awakens, sustains.

Owls, carved, feathered, brass,
whisper triple wisdom.
Sometimes I listen.

Bronze Chinese horse's hooves exalt earth.
Sky flies his mane, tail.
Perfect form draws worship.

Jade-eyed cat, delicate, precise
as marks on paper, brushes whiskers
along my cheek. We feel our way to light.

# Perspectives on Zero

Zero, man-made abstraction
like God and infinity
encompasses void
or a rose window mandala.

In deep space, astronomers believe
there is no nothing.
Black holes feed on light.
Pulsars spin gravity waves.

Yin and yang, yes and no
click computer switches, control minds.
Zero sum strategies maximize gain,
minimize loss, abstract human behavior.

Love arcs where Eros aims.
From golden center, circles expand
from zero to infinity,
sounding shores in small pools.

Music begins between circles of sound.
Bow motion on cello strings
accents air within silence,
celebrates sorrow, exaltation.

There is reason to believe
that zero contains all that may be:
cone shape vanishes to black;
white light prisms into rainbow.

# OBSERVATORY

Saturn's rings, Jupiter's moons
leap at my eye from the lens:
telescoped time
distance thrown awry.

Do I distort the universe
with my inquisitive eye?

Space expands to fill the sky available.
Stars are peepholes in black fabric.
Wormholes, unseen, contract
wandering matter into nothing.
Theoretical constructs
of terrifying implications
scare astronomers numberless.

Standing uncertain on earth's thin skin
axis wobbling
molten core sloshing
we stumble through space.

# GEOMETRY LESSON

The first form is a circle:
Sun, moon, the elementals,
mandala, the wheel of yang and yin.
Add a few lines, make a cone,
a paper drinking cup.

The next form is a square:
like a child draws a house
more precise than irregular cave mouth.
Make extra lines for a cube
and you're boxed in.

Then there is the triangle,
which rarely occurs in nature,
means eternal tragedy when you get caught
in complicated loves that won't fit
into calm circles or righteous squares.

The triangle is an ominous form.
It doubles to a cutting diamond, becomes trapezoids,
pentagons, any number of threatening shapes.
I'd avoid it if I were you.
You might get lost in the ramifications.

# CLOSE-UP

Paradox: I create space
drawing a mud puddle.
I feel like Blake. (He drew God.)
His grains of sand translate
to significance beyond what's known
to less than gods.

Sand is a sure thing on ocean shores.
Mud puddles dry up, become dust.
I'll visit it again tomorrow before rain
to work on the drawing. Someone
will have thrown stones in my puddle,
trod on it, messed it up.

This landscape is not mine. Yet
the ever-changing portrait of myself,
drawn in colors mixed with fate and care,
mirrored in mud, reflected in water,
delineates expanding space,
shifting sands, immensity of sky.

# SPROUTS

I rinse the seeds and watch.
On the third day, tails appear,
delicate tendrils sprung from dormancy.

I dreamed of sprouts last night,
tails twined like snakes.
I sprouted long-coveted tail.

Too old to grow unlike myself,
I'll spin new tales, weave snake spells,
travel in trees with monkeys.

Dream tales seed their own stories.
Thereby hangs another tail:
monkey business all around.

When tale is told, I waken cold,
longing for a different tale:
funny as monkeys, alive as sprouts.

# Animal, Vegetable, Mineral

I am juniper,
roots twisted, stretched
in search of water.
I am sandstone,
weathered by relentless wind.

I am sieve, funnel, soup pot,
simmering herbs, greens, meat,
to my own recipe, life-tested,
mind-flavored succulent stew.

I am owl, ant, lioness
on the prowl. I fly, feast, growl,
grovel, ponder the ways of prey,
comply with the moon.

# VISION

There's a Tyger in my tom

No
Not like Blake's beast
Really

Yet
archetypal there
under twenty pounds of fur

domestic
docile
with ten years
sleeping by the fire

I saw
stalking
across a cultured lawn
darkening to mystery

A Cat form

pausing
arched set to spring

primordial pose
intense symmetry

# STORM

Nothing new on a rainy night.
Trees catch water in new leaves
now the wind is still. Every April
for ten thousand years, peach blossoms
blow apart from their stems,
cruel storms tear at their roots.

Trees must stand their ground,
no dancing away from danger, no
panic rush to a safe place,
no safe place. They must stand
and take the storm as it comes,
the brunt of it on green buds.

# Two Views of T'ang Landscape

I'll imitate Li Po
   drink wine
   drown diving for the moon
   swim in snow
   up to my ears in bananas

I can't hear
I have a banana in my ear

They say in Ch'ang-an flowers bloom all year
Lovers wander by the fragrant shores
Tiger makes merry with the hare
The Emperor has bananas on the brain

Peach blossom spring is late this year
Landscape blurs with winter rain
Snow stipples grass, wind churns river
Logic freezes and nothing feels sane

I'll imitate Tu Fu
   ponder dying
   study Confucius
   praise paintings
   turn trim quatrains true

The Emperor has a banana in his ear
Who will hear?

# My Frog

Ancient Chinese bronze
cool to my kiss,
you need no prince inside.

I rub your back
you wink at me, wit
survived a thousand years.

I caress your webbed toes,
watch your lips
anticipate the taste of fly.

Did whoever made you know
my loving touch
would spring your eye to lively gleam?

# MOUNT ST. HELENS: EASTER, 1980

*St. Helen was the Emperor Constantine's mother. She discovered the True Cross. The mountain bore a rock cross, now obscured by ash.*

I lie along the fault.
I have slept too long
entombed in Adam's error.
I think I will erupt now.

Arrhythmic heart tumbles skiers
from my lower slopes.
Lakes, summer homes shiver.
Timber, rocks tremble.

Where is your god now,
harmonic Constantine?
You won't find the true cross
balanced along your sword.

Ashes spew from my breast,
no more kind milk, nurturing,
just dust apples, dead sea fruit
sterile mud, wormwood.

Once encased in ice,
molten rock now rumbles my belly.
Snow explodes from my heaving thighs.
Blue lightning arcs my navel crater.

94

Sulphur contaminates my lake,
Lava describes a new cross
seismic skeleton ripped of soil.
Beware the earth-sword, Constantine.

# BETWEEN THE WORLDS

Journeys, motion among spaces—
what fills space between edges?
We shift and grind; tectonic plates
make earthquakes, angry edges
rub to smoothness betweenness.

Spaced, shaped, this mark on white paper
is black, means me who makes it,
edge on both sides of it, but Oh,
this white is so silent, demands,
taunts, tortures this pen to
do something, create, come on you

fool, why can't you make something
beautiful? What were you born for,
anyway? Breed and die, or go
sterile into that black night that
knows no edge, nor shape, nor time.

Motion along the edge of it, take care:
Journey with luggage intact,
passport, necessary medications,
credit cards, travelers' checks,
first-class accommodations in the best hotels.
Not farewell, but fare forward, voyagers.

# EDGE OF ALONE

Uneasy at rest
Poised on a continent's westernmost edge
Lips taste of salt
Here on the sere edge of alone

The city builds behind me
A garden surrounds

   line drawn in the gray light
   a fine Chinese brush
   tracing each moist leaf
   with a delicate hand

   essence of texture and shape
   washed hint of green
   tang scent of dewed leaves
   sound of the sea below

A garden enclosed
Safe from the edge of alone

# DIARY OF DRAWING LILACS

Early April when life
had hardly begun, lines were clear,
not taxing my budding skill.

May Day, burgeoning leaves
made complex shapes of light and shade.
What were once easy, familiar shapes

had grown beyond drawing, passed
beyond knowing with my simple pencil
faltering above a flat white page.

Late May, lilac burst their bounds.
I cannot capture fragrance, hue.
Freed from green sheathes, flowers

fling scent to the wind. My art
has not kept pace with their growing.
Aspiring spirit seeks their essence.

# DEMOISELLE d'ARBRE

Tree lady, leaf eyed, twig-mouthed,
you change with each wind
as November destroys us.

I wake each morning,
find your face through the window,
take on the mood your eyebrows invite.

You are my day's omen, my sister
outside. Picasso splintered you.
I put you together within me.

As Druids did, I revere you.
Lady of Trees, your hair
is wind-driven leaf clouds,

your roots hold earth in her orbit,
your tears are the rain.
Your bud-breasts promise rebirth.

# Goddess: A Cycle of Celebration

HALLOWEEN

> Moon Lady, mother of tides,
> you circle the seasons around you.
> White witch magic comforts all souls.
>
> We sense your spirit within us,
> Earth-keeper, your hair streams
> in wind-driven clouds.

CANDLEMAS

> Snow Lady, you've aged,
> tree form heavy laden, earth-bent,
> withered eyes clouded with white.
>
> Amaryllis shaft thrusts burgeoning bud,
> spreads red wings against grayness,
> proof that your magic begins.
>
> Under earth in dark, live caves of soil,
> seeds stir, awaken,
> summoned again to your circle of light.

MAY DAY

> Lilac Lady, spring breath dances your buds,
> whispers pines in suppleness.
> Snow recedes from your sun-smile.

Birth time:  Pan pipes each morning,
evoking miracles of green.
Bees compete for your sweetness.

Ancient Earth Lady, reborn,
crowned in regalia of flowers,
your promises all performed.


## MIDSUMMER

Thor's thunder is silenced.
Lilac leaves rustle in clear air.
Moon commands the evening sky.

Your hands, feather wind,
massage my forehead. You whisper
"Yes," with the crickets.

I drew your portrait long ago;
Earth Mother, wheat-crowned,
magic, gray-robed, unknown.

Here again in your circle of daughters,
our voices chime with bells,
nightingales song in twilit trees.

We, all One, among flowers,
maiden, mother, crone,
celebrate, worship our lives.

## LAMMASTIDE

Corn Lady, we feast on first fruits
from your bounty of seed and rain.
Grapes ripen on heavy vines.

Shadows lengthen across green fields.
Chill evening air reminds us
earth's wheel forever turns,

spirals to new knowing.

# To the Moon

Moon sister, mother of tides
giver of sleep and dreams
moving softly through winter skies
lover of evening wind.

You bring life to the clouds
wandering limitless space
lost without your light.

You wax and wane and wax again
knowing your seasons
the tides of your body
the flow of calm night.

You rise between canyon sides
spread to accept your ascent
to the sky.

# GENERATION

Disguise pretends you are not there.
Designed to fade into trees, sand, swamp,
patterned-colored skin hides you.

Avoiding encounter on rainy night,
you imagine images, crouch alone on your branch.
Lightning menaces, thought congeals.

Instinct, memory grow slowly,
leave fossils behind,
instruct the carapace you need

to defend against surge of tide,
carnivore teeth, snake threat,
in pond's depth you inhabit.

You acquire flexible hands, legs,
creep out of water, rise erect on new land.
You tame fire, learn skill, draw suns:

incantation of life not stilled.
You survive aware with pen and brush,
create patterns to keep you alive.

# COLLECTION

Of woman born, a woman
I was passed from father
to husband to sons,
nurturer of plants and cats
alien, at peace for a time.

Now the stars have shifted courses
passage strange horizons.
I hear my sisters singing
a different song.

A closer look at Ariel
captive in her dying tree:
an ordinary woman grows
no revolutionary petunias.
They thrive in my study:
sunflower splendor
of nine songs.

After Babel, the distances
and then the quiet time
growing a grain of mustard seed
at rest on a wandering star.

# Artist's Conception

Sound without ears, unheard:
there is no one here
to listen for wind chimes
strung in set landscape.

Everything is still:
house without windows
trees motionless
sky without clouds.

Silent discs hang
from captured driftwood.
Leather thong attached
to nowhere in space.

What do I mean, who made it?
Amateur, remembering child dream
of colored pencils
abandoned for easier toys.

Awakened color complements
vision inscribed in black words
on white paper, resonates
even when wind is still.

# WINTER IS NOT FOR WOMEN

Sickle moon rose on Christ-mas Eve,
dark circle sunset shaped,
more yin than yang,
light sliver.
Venus wheeled above, no ease

surcease on Solstice nights.
Survivors for this time,
we whisper together,
one friend in black pain, another dead.
We mourn, look for the moon,
hidden under arrant clouds.

# LITA AND THE CROW

We make our own mythologies.
Hercules occurs, recurs
riding carousel horses, cyclic.
Only heroism invents, renews.

Danaë's shower of gold exists
weaving among Forms,
one heroine reborn,
older than oldest hills.

One day, a New Thing,
phoenix with rainbow wings,
rises above shellac,
gesso, charcoal, newsprint,

from minds livened, shaken
away from usual circles of drawing.
Model meets Bird; strange stories are born,
amber, heroic and true.

# ABOUT OWLS

Athene whispers
make friends with an owl

For victory
release an owl

Owl on the mountain
no earthquake

Bronze owl winks through museum glass
I laugh back

Coyote and owl trick each other
who will win

Owl cries while crickets sing
death does not matter

I dream free flight
searching for owls

# Alice Gorton Hart

Alice Gorton was born in 1932 in Cleveland, Ohio, and spent a happy but restless childhood there with her mother and father, Gee and Douglas, and her younger brother, Bill. It was a comfortable life with reading, sports, and dating in pleasing proportions.

At Smith College in the early 1950s Alice enjoyed the fulfillment of her intellectual promise as well as the contemporary social whirl of a young girl growing to womanhood. This transition is documented in her personal journals which record the exceptional record of this extraordinary woman from her teen years to her death. Her journals and poetry are now housed in the Sophia Smith Collection at Smith College.

Alice Gorton put aside dreams of graduate school when she met and married a forester named George Hart. His career took them to Michigan, West Virginia, New Hampshire, and finally Logan, Utah. There she obtained her Master of Arts degree in English from Utah State University in 1970. She was an inspired teacher and proudly taught part-time in Utah State University's English department for many years.

It was in Logan that Alice truly grew as a poet, artist, and most importantly, as a woman who was truly sensitive to the needs of others as she sought to understand how she fit into the larger picture of family, friends, society, universe. She mothered her two sons, David and Andrew, and rejoiced in their growing-up years. She mentored others as well and enhanced her own growing patterns. She was a seeker and a giver and combined the two seamlessly.

In her writing, poetry, and painting Alice loved the process of creation seemingly more than the production. It was the touch of pen on white paper, the whisper of pastel on a clean drawing sheet, the mind focusing on ideas: these were of essence to Alice. The publications, the art shows, the awards...these were nice but the mere end-products of the creative process.

Alice died suddenly in the spring of 1987 following cancer therapy. This book commemorates her life and the unique flowing facets of her personality. Through the reading of the poems, both the reader and Alice are able "To Fly Once More."

Composed in 11.5/15 point Varityper 6400
Times Roman with 18 and 14 point
condensed Times Roman display by
Utah State University Publication Design
and Production, Logan, Utah. Printed sheet-
fed offset by Woodruff Printing Company,
Salt Lake City, Utah, on Monadnock Dulcet
Text, smooth finish, Basis 80. Bound by
Hiller Industries, Salt Lake City, Utah,
in Van Heek Brillianta book cloth with
Rainbow Antique Willow endpapers.

Limited edition of 400 copies.